# Cake Mix Magic

# Baking Secrets

## The Basics

It doesn't take a magician to make delicious treats! Simply follow these guidelines for successful baking.

• Read the entire recipe before beginning to make sure you have all the necessary ingredients and baking utensils.

• Remove butter, margarine and cream cheese from the refrigerator to soften, if necessary.

• Toast and chop nuts, pare and slice fruit, and melt chocolate before preparing the batter or dough.

• Measure all the ingredients accurately and assemble them in the order they are called for in the recipe.

• Always use the pan size specified in the recipe, and prepare the pan as directed in the recipe.

• When substituting glass bakeware in recipes that call for baking pans, reduce the oven temperature by 25°F.

• Adjust the oven racks and preheat the oven. Check the oven temperature for accuracy with an oven thermometer.

# The Perfect Pan

**Baking Pan:** Metal baking pans are square, rectangular or round, and have straight sides at least 1½ inches high. The most common sizes are 8- and 9-inch square or round; 11×7×2 inches; and 13×9×2 inches. Baking pans (sometimes referred to as cake pans) are designed for cakes and bar cookies. Shiny aluminum pans are ideal for producing a tender, lightly browned cake crust.

**Baking Sheet:** A baking sheet (often referred to as a cookie sheet) is a flat, rigid sheet of metal on which stiff dough is baked into cookies, rolls, biscuits, etc. It has a low lip on one or more sides for ease in handling; a lip higher than one-half inch interferes with surface browning, especially of cookies. The type of surface also determines the browning characteristics of the baking sheet. Shiny finishes promote even browning. Dark metal baking sheets absorb more heat and can cause food to brown too quickly. Insulated baking sheets have a layer of air sandwiched between two sheets of aluminum which helps to prevent excess browning, but increases baking time. (Some cookie doughs may also spread more on these sheets.) Nonstick finishes minimize sticking and make cleanup easier.

# Measuring Magic

**Dry Ingredients:** Always use standardized measuring spoons and cups. Fill the appropriate measuring spoon or cup to overflowing, and level it off with a metal spatula or the flat edge of a knife.

**Liquid Ingredients:** Use a standardized glass or plastic measuring cup with a pouring spout and calibrations marked on the side. Place the cup on a flat surface, fill to the desired mark, and check the measurement at eye level.

# Charming Classics

## Brownie Cake Delight

**1 package fudge brownie mix**
**⅓ cup strawberry all-fruit spread**
**2 cups thawed nondairy whipped topping**
**¼ teaspoon almond extract**
**2 cups strawberries, stems removed, halved**
**¼ cup chocolate sauce**

*1.* Prepare brownies according to package directions, substituting 11×7-inch baking pan. Cool. Whisk fruit spread in small bowl until smooth. Combine whipped topping and almond extract in bowl.

*2.* Cut brownie horizontally in half. Place half of brownie on serving dish. Spread with fruit spread and 1 cup whipped topping. Place second half of brownie, cut side down, over bottom layer. Spread with remaining whipped topping. Place strawberries on whipped topping. Drizzle chocolate sauce over cake before serving.

*Makes 16 servings*
*Brownie Cake Delight*

## Boston Cream Pie

½ **package light yellow cake mix**
⅛ **teaspoon baking soda**
⅔ **cup water**
2 **egg whites**
1½ **teaspoons vanilla, divided**
1 **package (3⅜ ounces) sugar-free instant vanilla pudding mix**
1⅓ **cups skim milk**
**Chocolate Glaze (recipe follows)**

*1.* Preheat oven to 350°F. Spray 9-inch round cake pan with nonstick cooking spray. Lightly coat with flour. Set aside.

*2.* Combine cake mix and baking soda in large bowl; mix well. Add water, egg whites and 1 teaspoon vanilla. Beat at low speed with electric mixer 30 seconds. Increase speed to medium; beat 2 minutes.

*3.* Pour batter into prepared pan. Bake 30 minutes or until cake pulls away from side of pan and springs back when touched lightly in center. Remove from oven. Cool 10 minutes on wire rack. Invert onto serving plate; cool completely.

*4.* Combine pudding mix, milk and remaining ½ teaspoon vanilla in bowl. Beat at low speed with electric mixer 2 minutes; set aside.

*5.* Prepare Chocolate Glaze.

*6.* Cut cake in half horizontally; carefully remove top half of cake. Spread bottom half with pudding mixture. Replace top half; spoon Chocolate Glaze over top. Allow to stand until glaze hardens. Cut into wedges.

*Makes 8 servings*

## Chocolate Glaze

⅔ **cup powdered sugar**
1 **tablespoon unsweetened cocoa powder**
1 **tablespoon water**
½ **teaspoon vanilla**

*1.* Sift together powdered sugar and cocoa in medium bowl. Add water and vanilla; mix well.

*2.* Add more water, 1 teaspoon at a time, until desired spreading consistency.

*Boston Cream Pie*

## Streusel Coffeecake

**32 CHIPS AHOY!® Chocolate
  Chip Cookies, divided
1 (18- to 18.5-ounce) package
  yellow or white cake mix
½ cup sour cream
½ cup PLANTERS® Pecans,
  chopped
½ cup flaked coconut
¼ cup packed brown sugar
1 teaspoon ground cinnamon
⅓ cup butter, melted
  Powdered sugar glaze,
  optional**

*1.* Coarsely chop 20 cookies;
finely crush remaining 12 cookies.
Set aside.

*2.* Prepare cake mix batter
according to package directions;
stir in sour cream and chopped
cookies. Pour into greased and
floured 13×9×2-inch baking pan.

*3.* Mix cookie crumbs, pecans,
coconut, brown sugar and
cinnamon. Stir in butter; sprinkle
over cake batter.

*4.* Bake at 350°F for 40 minutes
or until toothpick inserted in center
of cake comes out clean. Cool
completely. Drizzle with glaze, if
desired.      *Makes 24 servings*

## Swiss Chocolate Crispies

**1 package DUNCAN HINES®
  Moist Deluxe® Swiss
  Chocolate Cake Mix
½ cup shortening plus
  additional for greasing
½ cup butter or margarine,
  softened
2 eggs
2 tablespoons water
3 cups crispy rice cereal,
  divided**

*1.* Combine cake mix, ½ cup
shortening, butter, eggs and water
in large bowl. Beat at low speed
with electric mixer for 2 minutes.
Fold in 1 cup cereal. Refrigerate
1 hour.

*2.* Crush remaining 2 cups cereal
into coarse crumbs.

*3.* Preheat oven to 350°F. Grease
cookie sheets. Shape dough into
1-inch balls. Roll in crushed
cereal. Place on cookie sheets
about 1 inch apart.

*4.* Bake 11 to 13 minutes. Cool
1 minute on cookie sheets.
Remove to wire racks.
      *Makes 4 dozen cookies*

*Streusel Coffeecake*

## Pineapple Upside Down Cake

### Topping
- ½ **cup butter or margarine**
- 1 **cup firmly packed brown sugar**
- 1 **can (20 ounces) pineapple slices, well drained**
- **Maraschino cherries, halved and drained**
- **Walnut halves**

### Cake
- 1 **package DUNCAN HINES® Moist Deluxe® Pineapple Supreme Cake Mix**
- 1 **package (4-serving size) vanilla instant pudding and pie filling mix**
- 4 **eggs**
- 1 **cup water**
- ½ **cup oil**

*1.* Preheat oven to 350°F.

*2.* For topping, melt butter over low heat in 12-inch cast-iron skillet or skillet with oven-proof handle. Remove from heat. Stir in brown sugar. Spread to cover bottom of skillet. Arrange pineapple slices, maraschino cherries and walnut halves in skillet. Set aside.

*3.* For cake, combine cake mix, pudding mix, eggs, water and oil in large mixing bowl. Beat at medium speed with electric mixer for 2 minutes. Pour batter evenly over fruit in skillet. Bake at 350°F for 1 hour or until toothpick inserted in center comes out clean. Invert onto serving plate.

*Makes 16 to 20 servings*

### Magical Tip

*This cake can also be made in a 13×9×2-inch pan. Bake at 350°F for 45 to 55 minutes or until a toothpick inserted into the center comes out clean.*

*Pineapple Upside Down Cake*

# Crispy Thumbprint Cookies

1 package (18.25 ounces)
   yellow cake mix
1/2 cup vegetable oil
1/4 cup water
1 egg
3 cups crisp rice cereal,
   crushed
1/2 cup chopped walnuts
6 tablespoons raspberry
   preserves

*1.* Preheat oven to 375°F.

*2.* Combine cake mix, oil, water and egg. Beat at medium speed of electric mixer until well blended. Add cereal and walnuts; mix until well blended.

*3.* Drop by heaping teaspoonfuls 2 inches apart onto ungreased baking sheets. Use thumb to make indentation in each cookie. Spoon about 1/2 teaspoon preserves into center of each cookie.

*4.* Bake 9 to 11 minutes or until golden brown. Cool cookies 1 minute on baking sheet; remove from baking sheet to wire rack to cool completely.

*Makes 3 dozen cookies*

# Golden Gingersnaps

1 package DUNCAN HINES®
   Golden Sugar Cookie Mix
1 egg
1 tablespoon water
1 tablespoon light molasses
1 1/2 teaspoons ground ginger
1 teaspoon ground cinnamon
1/2 teaspoon baking soda
1/4 cup granulated sugar
1 tablespoon milk
1/3 cup finely chopped pecans

*1.* Preheat oven to 375°F. Grease cookie sheets.

*2.* Combine cookie mix, egg, water, molasses, ginger, cinnamon and baking soda in large bowl. Stir until thoroughly blended. Drop by level tablespoonfuls into sugar. Roll to completely cover. Place 2 inches apart on prepared cookie sheets. Flatten slightly with bottom of drinking glass. Brush tops lightly with milk. Sprinkle with pecans. Bake 9 minutes for chewy cookies or 10 minutes for crisp cookies. Cool 2 minutes on cookie sheets. Remove to cooling racks. Cool completely. Store in airtight container.

*Makes 3 dozen cookies*

*Crispy Thumbprint Cookies*

# Abracadabra Cakes

### Celebration Pumpkin Cake

  1 package (18 ounces) spice cake mix
  1 can (16 ounces) pumpkin
  3 eggs
  ¼ cup butter, softened
1½ tubs (16 ounces each) cream cheese frosting
  ⅓ cup caramel ice cream topping
     Pecan halves for garnish

Preheat oven to 350°F. Grease and flour 3 (9-inch) round cake pans. Combine cake mix, pumpkin, eggs and butter in bowl; beat 2 minutes. Divide batter among prepared pans. Bake 20 to 25 minutes or until toothpick inserted in centers comes out clean. Cool 5 minutes on wire rack. Remove from pans; cool completely. Place one cake layer on serving plate; top with frosting. Repeat layers, ending with frosting. Frost cake side. Spread caramel over cake top. Garnish with pecans.          *Makes 16 servings*

*Celebration Pumpkin Cake*

## Fudgy Ripple Cake

1 package (18.25 ounces)
    yellow cake mix plus
    ingredients to prepare mix
1 package (3 ounces) cream
    cheese, softened
2 tablespoons unsweetened
    cocoa powder
    Fudgy Glaze (recipe follows)
½ cup "M&M's"® Chocolate
    Mini Baking Bits

Preheat oven to 350°F. Grease and flour 10-inch bundt pan; set aside. Prepare cake batter as package directs. In bowl mix 1½ cups batter, cream cheese and cocoa powder until smooth. Pour half of yellow batter into prepared pan. Drop spoonfuls of chocolate batter over yellow batter in pan. Top with remaining yellow batter. Bake about 45 minutes or until toothpick inserted in center comes out clean. Cool on wire rack.

Invert cake onto serving plate. Prepare Fudgy Glaze; spread over cake, allowing some to run over side. Sprinkle with "M&M's"® Chocolate Mini Baking Bits.

*Makes 10 servings*

## Fudgy Glaze

1 square (1 ounce) semi-sweet
    chocolate
1 cup powdered sugar
⅓ cup unsweetened cocoa
    powder
3 tablespoons milk
½ teaspoon vanilla extract

Place chocolate in small microwave-safe bowl. Microwave at HIGH 30 seconds; stir. Repeat as necessary until chocolate is melted, stirring at 10-second intervals; set aside. In medium bowl combine powdered sugar and cocoa powder. Stir in milk, vanilla and chocolate until smooth.

### Magical Tip

*To soften cream cheese quickly, remove it from the wrapper and place it on a microwave-safe plate. Microwave at MEDIUM (50% power) 15 to 20 seconds or until softened.*

*Fudgy Ripple Cake*

# Black and White Pistachio Cake

### Cake

- 1 package (18¼ ounces) marble cake mix
- 3 eggs
- 1¼ cups water
- ⅓ cup vegetable oil
- ½ teaspoon vanilla

### Filling

- 2 packages (4-serving size each) pistachio instant pudding and pie filling mix
- 3 cups milk
- ⅓ cup chopped maraschino cherries, drained
- ¼ cup chopped pistachio nuts

### Frosting

- 1¼ cups cold milk
- 1 package (4-serving size) pistachio instant pudding and pie filling mix
- 2 envelopes whipped topping mix
  Additional maraschino cherries and pistachio nuts (optional)

### Cake

Preheat oven to 350°F. Lightly grease and flour two 8-inch round cake pans.

Combine cake mix, eggs, water, oil and vanilla in large bowl. Mix according to package directions. Spread half of batter in one pan. Stir contents of chocolate packet into remaining batter. Spread chocolate batter in second pan. Bake and cool according to package directions.

### Filling

Prepare pudding mixes using 3 cups milk. Stir in chopped cherries and pistachios. Cover and refrigerate until ready to use.

### Frosting

Combine milk, pudding mix and whipped topping mix in large bowl. Beat at low speed with electric mixer until blended. Beat at high speed 2 to 3 minutes or until stiff, scraping side of bowl often.

To assemble cake, split each cake layer in half. Alternate chocolate cake layer with white cake layer, spreading filling between each layer. Frost top and side of cake with frosting. Garnish with additional maraschino cherries and pistachios, if desired.

*Makes 12 to 16 servings*

*Black and White Pistachio Cake*

# Triple Chocolate Fantasy

### Cake

**1 package DUNCAN HINES®**
**Moist Deluxe® Devil's**
**Food Cake Mix**
**3 eggs**
**1⅓ cups water**
**½ cup vegetable oil**
**½ cup ground walnuts**

### Chocolate Glaze

**1 package (12 ounces)**
**semisweet chocolate chips**
**¼ cup plus 2 tablespoons**
**butter or margarine**
**¼ cup chopped walnuts**

### White Chocolate Glaze

**3 ounces white chocolate,**
**coarsely chopped**
**1 tablespoon shortening**

*1.* Preheat oven to 350°F. Grease and flour 10-inch Bundt® pan.

*2.* For cake, combine cake mix, eggs, water, oil and ground walnuts in large bowl. Beat for 2 minutes. Pour into pan.

*3.* Bake at 350°F 45 to 55 minutes or until toothpick inserted in center comes out clean. Cool in pan 25 minutes. Invert onto serving plate. Cool completely.

*4.* For chocolate glaze, combine chocolate chips and butter in small heavy saucepan. Heat on low heat until chips are melted. Stir constantly until shiny and smooth. (Glaze will be very thick.) Spread hot glaze over cooled cake. Sprinkle with chopped walnuts.

*5.* For white chocolate glaze, mix white chocolate and shortening in small heavy saucepan. Heat on low heat until melted, stirring constantly. Drizzle hot glaze over top and side of cake.

*Makes 12 to 16 servings*

## Magical Tip

*To reduce the risk of overprocessing when grinding nuts in a food processor, add a small amount of the flour or cake mix from the recipe. If they are overprocessed, nuts will become nut butter.*

*Triple Chocolate Fantasy*

# Magical Kids' Treats

## Chocolate Peanut Butter Cups

**1 package DUNCAN HINES® Moist Deluxe®
Swiss Chocolate Cake Mix**
**1 container DUNCAN HINES® Vanilla Frosting**
**½ cup creamy peanut butter**
**15 miniature peanut butter cup candies,
wrappers removed, cut in half vertically**

*1.* Preheat oven to 350°F. Place 30 (2½-inch) paper liners in muffin cups.

*2.* Prepare, bake and cool cupcakes following package directions for basic recipe.

*3.* Combine Vanilla frosting and peanut butter in medium bowl. Stir until smooth. Frost one cupcake. Decorate with peanut butter cup candy, cut-side down. Repeat with remaining cupcakes and candies.                *Makes 30 servings*


*Chocolate Peanut Butter Cups*

# I Think You're "Marbleous" Cupcakes

**1 box (18½ ounces) pudding-in-the-mix cake mix, any flavor**
**1¼ cups water**
**3 eggs**
**¼ cup oil**
**1 tub (16 ounces) vanilla frosting**
**1 tube (4¼ ounces) red decorating icing**

*1.* Preheat oven to 350°F. Grease or paper-line 24 (2½-inch) muffin cups. Prepare cake mix according to package directions with water, eggs and oil. Spoon batter into prepared cups, filling each ⅔ full.

*2.* Bake 20 to 25 minutes or until toothpick inserted into centers comes out clean. Cool in pans 20 minutes. Remove to wire rack; cool completely.

*3.* Spread 1½ to 2 tablespoons frosting over each cupcake. Fit one decorating round tip onto tube of icing. Squeeze 4 to 5 dots icing over each cupcake. Swirl toothpick through icing and frosting to marbleize or make heart shapes.

*Makes 2 dozen cupcakes*

# Double Nut Chocolate Chip Cookies

**1 package DUNCAN HINES® Moist Deluxe® Yellow Cake Mix**
**½ cup butter or margarine, melted**
**1 egg**
**1 cup semisweet chocolate chips**
**½ cup finely chopped pecans**
**1 cup sliced almonds, divided**

*1.* Preheat oven to 375°F. Grease cookie sheets.

*2.* Combine cake mix, butter and egg in large bowl. Mix at low speed with electric mixer until just blended. Stir in chocolate chips, pecans and ¼ cup almonds. Shape rounded tablespoonfuls of dough into balls. Place remaining ¾ cup almonds in shallow bowl. Press tops of cookies in almonds. Place 1 inch apart on prepared cookie sheets.

*3.* Bake 9 to 11 minutes or until lightly browned. Cool 2 minutes on cookie sheets. Remove to cooling racks.

*Makes 3 to 3½ dozen cookies*

*I Think You're "Marbleous" Cupcakes*

## Banana Split Cake

1 package DUNCAN HINES®
   Moist Deluxe® Banana
   Supreme Cake Mix
3 eggs
1⅓ cups water
½ cup all-purpose flour
⅓ cup vegetable oil
1 cup semi-sweet mini
   chocolate chips
2 to 3 bananas
1 can (16 ounces) chocolate
   syrup
1 container (8 ounces) frozen
   whipped topping, thawed
½ cup chopped walnuts
   Colored sprinkles
   Maraschino cherries with
   stems, for garnish

*1.* Preheat oven to 350°F. Grease and flour 13×9×2-inch pan.

*2.* Combine cake mix, eggs, water, flour and oil in large bowl. Beat at low speed with electric mixer until moistened. Beat at medium speed 2 minutes. Stir in chocolate chips. Pour into pan. Bake at 350°F 32 to 35 minutes or until toothpick inserted in center comes out clean. Cool completely.

*3.* Slice bananas. Cut cake into squares; top with banana slices.

Drizzle with chocolate syrup. Top with whipped topping, walnuts and sprinkles. Garnish with maraschino cherries.

*Makes 12 to 16 servings*

## Quick Peanut Butter Chocolate Chip Cookies

1 package DUNCAN HINES®
   Moist Deluxe® Classic
   Yellow Cake Mix
½ cup creamy peanut butter
½ cup butter or margarine,
   softened
2 eggs
1 cup milk chocolate chips

*1.* Preheat oven to 350°F. Grease cookie sheets.

*2.* Combine cake mix, peanut butter, butter and eggs in large bowl. Mix at low speed with electric mixer until blended. Stir in chocolate chips.

*3.* Drop by rounded teaspoonfuls onto prepared cookie sheets. Bake 9 to 11 minutes or until lightly browned. Cool 2 minutes on cookie sheets. Remove to cooling racks.

*Makes 4 dozen cookies*
*Banana Split Cake*

## *Boston Babies*

1 package (18¼ ounces)
    yellow cake mix
3 eggs *or* ¾ cup cholesterol-
    free egg substitute
⅓ cup unsweetened
    applesauce
1 package (4-serving size)
    sugar-free vanilla pudding
    and pie filling mix
2 cups low-fat (1%) milk or
    fat-free (skim) milk
⅓ cup sugar
⅓ cup unsweetened cocoa
    powder
1 tablespoon cornstarch
1½ cups water
1½ teaspoons vanilla

*1.* Line 24 (2½-inch) muffin cups with paper liners; set aside.

*2.* Prepare cake mix according to lower fat package directions, using 3 eggs and applesauce. Pour batter into prepared muffin cups. Bake according to package directions; cool completely. Freeze 12 cupcakes for another use.

*3.* Prepare pudding according to package directions, using 2 cups milk; cover and refrigerate.

*4.* Combine sugar, cocoa, cornstarch and water in large microwavable bowl; whisk until smooth. Microwave at HIGH 4 to 6 minutes, stirring every 2 minutes, until slightly thickened. Stir in vanilla.

*5.* To serve, drizzle 2 tablespoons chocolate glaze over each dessert plate. Cut cupcakes in half; place 2 halves on top of chocolate on each dessert plate. Top each with about 2 heaping tablespoonfuls pudding. Garnish if desired. Serve immediately.

*Makes 12 servings*

*Magical Tip*

*These treats are a great low-fat snack! Each serving has 158 calories and only 4 grams of fat.*

*Boston Baby*

## *Kids' Confetti Cake*

### *Cake*

- **1 package DUNCAN HINES® Moist Deluxe® Yellow Cake Mix**
- **1 package (4-serving size) vanilla instant pudding and pie filling mix**
- **4 eggs**
- **1 cup water**
- **½ cup vegetable oil**
- **1 cup semi-sweet mini chocolate chips**

### *Topping*

- **1 cup colored miniature marshmallows**
- **⅔ cup DUNCAN HINES® Chocolate Frosting**
- **2 tablespoons semi-sweet mini chocolate chips**

*1.* Preheat oven to 350°F. Lightly grease and flour 13×9×2-inch baking pan.

*2.* For cake, combine cake mix, pudding mix, eggs, water and oil in large bowl. Beat at medium speed with electric mixer 2 minutes. Stir in 1 cup chocolate chips. Pour into pan. Bake 40 to 45 minutes or until toothpick inserted in center comes out clean.

*3.* For topping, immediately arrange marshmallows evenly over hot cake. Place frosting in microwave-safe bowl. Microwave at HIGH (100% power) 25 to 30 seconds. Stir until smooth. Drizzle over marshmallows and cake. Sprinkle with 2 tablespoons chocolate chips. Cool completely.

*Makes 12 to 16 servings*

### *Magical Tip*

*To grease and flour cake pans, use a paper towel, waxed paper or your fingers to apply a thin, even layer of shortening. Sprinkle flour into the greased pan; shake or tilt the pan to coat evenly with flour, then tap lightly to remove any excess.*

*Kids' Confetti Cake*

# Quick-as-a-Wink Cookies

## Chocolate Chip 'n Oatmeal Cookies

1 package (18.25 or 18.5 ounces) yellow cake
    mix
1 cup quick-cooking rolled oats, uncooked
¾ cup butter or margarine, softened
2 eggs
1 cup HERSHEY¡S Semi-Sweet Chocolate Chips

1. Heat oven to 350°F.

2. Combine cake mix, oats, butter and eggs in large bowl; mix well. Stir in chocolate chips. Drop by rounded teaspoons onto ungreased cookie sheets.

3. Bake 10 to 12 minutes or until very lightly browned. Cool slightly; remove from cookie sheets to wire racks. Cool completely.

*Makes 4 dozen cookies*

*Chocolate Chip 'n Oatmeal Cookies*

## Cheesecake-Topped Brownies

- 1 (21- or 23.6-ounce) package fudge brownie mix
- 1 (8-ounce) package cream cheese, softened
- 2 tablespoons butter, softened
- 1 tablespoon cornstarch
- 1 (14-ounce) can EAGLE® BRAND Sweetened Condensed Milk (NOT evaporated milk)
- 1 egg
- 2 teaspoons vanilla extract
  Ready-to-spread chocolate frosting (optional)
  Orange peel (optional)

*1.* Preheat oven to 350°F. Prepare brownie mix as package directs. Spread in well-greased 13×9-inch baking pan.

*2.* Beat cream cheese, butter and cornstarch until fluffy. Beat in Eagle Brand, egg and vanilla until smooth. Pour cheesecake mixture over brownie batter.

*3.* Bake 40 to 45 minutes or until top is lightly browned. Cool. Spread with frosting or sprinkle with orange peel, if desired. Store covered in refrigerator.
*Makes 36 to 40 brownies*

## Banana Chocolate Chip Cookies

- 2 extra-ripe, medium DOLE® Bananas, peeled
- 1 package (17.5 ounces) chocolate chip cookie mix
- ½ teaspoon ground cinnamon
- 1 egg, lightly beaten
- 1 teaspoon vanilla extract
- 1 cup toasted wheat germ

• Mash bananas with fork. Measure 1 cup.

• Combine cookie mix and cinnamon. Stir in contents of enclosed flavoring packet, mashed bananas, egg and vanilla until well blended. Stir in wheat germ.

• Drop batter by heaping tablespoonfuls 2 inches apart onto cookie sheets coated with cooking spray. Shape cookies with back of spoon. Bake in 375°F oven 10 to 12 minutes until lightly browned. Cool on wire racks.
*Makes 18 cookies*

*Cheesecake-Topped Brownies*

## Coconut Clouds

**2⅔ cups flaked coconut, divided**
**1 package DUNCAN HINES®**
    **Moist Deluxe® Yellow**
    **Cake Mix**
**1 egg**
**½ cup vegetable oil**
**¼ cup water**
**1 teaspoon almond extract**

*1.* Preheat oven to 350°F. Place 1⅓ cups coconut in medium bowl; set aside.

*2.* Combine cake mix, egg, oil, water and almond extract in large bowl. Beat at low speed with electric mixer. Stir in remaining 1⅓ cups reserved coconut. Drop rounded teaspoonful dough into reserved coconut. Roll to cover lightly. Place on ungreased baking sheet. Repeat with remaining dough, placing balls 2 inches apart.

*3.* Bake at 350°F 10 to 12 minutes or until light golden brown. Let cool 1 minute on baking sheets. Remove to cooling racks. Cool completely. Store in airtight container.

*Makes 3½ dozen cookies*

*Coconut Clouds*

# Chocolate Caramel Pecan Squares

**1 (14-ounce) package caramels, unwrapped**
**²⁄₃ cup evaporated milk, divided**
**1 (18.25-ounce) package German chocolate cake mix (pudding style)**
**½ cup butter, melted**
**1 (6-ounce) package semi-sweet chocolate chips**
**1 cup chopped pecans, divided**

Preheat oven to 350°F. Melt caramels with ⅓ cup evaporated milk in saucepan over low heat until smooth, stirring often. Combine cake mix, butter and remaining ⅓ cup evaporated milk. Press half of cake mixture into greased 13×9-inch baking pan. Bake 6 minutes. Remove from oven. Sprinkle top with chocolate chips and ½ cup pecans. Top with caramel mixture, spreading to edges of pan. Spoon remaining cake mixture over top and sprinkle with remaining ½ cup pecans. Bake 20 minutes. Cut into squares. Serve warm or cool completely.

*Makes 24 squares*

# Peanut Butter Marbled Brownies

**4 ounces cream cheese, softened**
**½ cup peanut butter**
**2 tablespoons sugar**
**1 egg**
**1 package (20 to 22 ounces) brownie mix plus ingredients to prepare mix**
**¾ cup lightly salted cocktail peanuts**

• Preheat oven to 350°F. Grease 13×9-inch baking pan; set aside.

• Beat cream cheese, peanut butter, sugar and egg in medium bowl until blended.

• Prepare brownie mix according to package directions. Spread brownie batter in prepared pan. Spoon peanut butter mixture in dollops over batter; swirl with tip of knife. Sprinkle peanuts on top; lightly press into batter.

• Bake 30 to 35 minutes or until toothpick inserted into center comes out almost clean. Do not overbake. Cool in pan on wire rack. Cut into 2-inch squares.

*Makes 2 dozen brownies*

## Festive Fudge Blossoms

¼ cup butter, softened
1 box (18.25 ounces) chocolate fudge cake mix
1 egg, slightly beaten
2 tablespoons water
¾ to 1 cup finely chopped walnuts
48 chocolate star candies

*1.* Preheat oven to 350°F. Cut butter into cake mix in large bowl until mixture resembles coarse crumbs. Stir in egg and water until well blended.

*2.* Shape dough into ½-inch balls; roll in walnuts, pressing nuts gently into dough. Place about 2 inches apart on ungreased baking sheets.

*3.* Bake cookies 12 minutes or until puffed and nearly set. Place chocolate star candy in center of each cookie; bake 1 minute. Cool about 2 minutes on baking sheet. Remove cookies from baking sheets to wire rack to cool completely.

*Makes 4 dozen cookies*

**Prep and Bake Time:** 30 minutes

## Apricot Crumb Squares

1 package (18.25 ounces) light yellow cake mix
1 teaspoon ground cinnamon
½ teaspoon ground nutmeg
6 tablespoons cold butter, cut into pieces
¾ cup uncooked multigrain oatmeal cereal
1 whole egg
2 egg whites
1 tablespoon water
1 jar (10 ounces) apricot fruit spread
2 tablespoons firmly packed light brown sugar

• Preheat oven to 350°F. Combine cake mix, cinnamon and nutmeg in bowl. Cut in butter with pastry blender until coarse crumbs form. Stir in cereal. Reserve 1 cup mixture. Mix egg, egg whites and water into remaining mixture.

• Spread batter in ungreased 13×9-inch baking pan. Top with fruit spread; sprinkle with reserved mixture. Top with brown sugar.

• Bake 35 to 40 minutes or until golden brown. Cool in pan on wire rack. *Makes 15 squares*

*Festive Fudge Blossoms*

## Cinnamon Stars

**2 tablespoons sugar**
**¾ teaspoon ground cinnamon**
**¾ cup butter or margarine,
softened**
**2 egg yolks**
**1 teaspoon vanilla extract**
**1 package DUNCAN HINES®
Moist Deluxe® French
Vanilla Cake Mix**

*1.* Preheat oven to 375°F.
Combine sugar and cinnamon in
small bowl. Set aside.

*2.* Combine butter, egg yolks and
vanilla extract in large bowl.
Blend in cake mix gradually. Roll
to ⅛-inch thickness on lightly
floured surface. Cut with 2½-inch
star cookie cutter. Place 2 inches
apart on ungreased baking sheet.

*3.* Sprinkle cookies with
cinnamon-sugar mixture. Bake at
375°F for 6 to 8 minutes or until
edges are light golden brown.
Cool 1 minute on baking sheet.
Remove to cooling rack. Cool
completely. Store in airtight
container.

*Makes 3 to 3½ dozen
cookies*

## Fudgy Oatmeal Butterscotch Cookies

**1 package (18.25 ounces)
devil's food cake mix**
**1½ cups quick-cooking or
old-fashioned oats,
uncooked**
**¾ cup (1½ sticks) butter,
melted**
**2 large eggs**
**1 tablespoon vegetable oil**
**1 teaspoon vanilla extract**
**1¼ cups "M&M's"® Chocolate
Mini Baking Bits**
**1 cup butterscotch chips**

Preheat oven to 350°F. In large
bowl combine cake mix, oats,
butter, eggs, oil and vanilla until
well blended. Stir in "M&M's"®
Chocolate Mini Baking Bits and
butterscotch chips. Drop by
heaping tablespoonfuls 2 inches
apart onto ungreased cookie
sheets. Bake 10 to 12 minutes.
Cool 1 minute on cookie sheets;
cool completely on wire racks.
Store in tightly covered container.

*Makes 3 dozen cookies*

*Cinnamon Stars*

## Quick Chocolate Softies

**1 package (18.25 ounces)
   devil's food cake mix**
**1/3 cup water**
**1/4 cup butter, softened**
**1 egg**
**1 cup white chocolate baking
   chips**
**1/2 cup coarsely chopped
   walnuts**

• Preheat oven to 350°F. Grease cookie sheets. Combine cake mix, water, butter and egg in large bowl. Beat with electric mixer at low speed until moistened. Increase speed to medium; beat 1 minute. (Dough will be thick.) Stir in white chocolate chips and nuts; mix until well blended. Drop dough by heaping teaspoonfuls 2 inches apart onto prepared cookie sheets.

• Bake 10 to 12 minutes or until set. Let cookies stand on cookie sheets 1 minute. Remove cookies to wire racks; cool completely.

*Makes 4 dozen cookies*

## Maple Walnut Bars

**1 package DUNCAN HINES®
   Moist Deluxe® Classic
   Yellow Cake Mix, divided**
**1/3 cup butter, melted**
**4 eggs, divided**
**1 1/3 cups MRS. BUTTERWORTH®
   Maple Syrup**
**1/3 cup packed light brown
   sugar**
**1/2 teaspoon vanilla extract**
**1 cup chopped walnuts**

*1.* Preheat oven to 350°F. Grease 13×9-inch pan.

*2.* Reserve 2/3 cup cake mix; set aside. Combine remaining cake mix, melted butter and 1 egg in large bowl. Stir until thoroughly blended. (Mixture will be crumbly.) Press into prepared pan. Bake 15 to 20 minutes or until light golden brown.

*3.* Combine reserved cake mix, maple syrup, remaining 3 eggs, sugar and vanilla in large bowl. Beat at low speed with electric mixer for 3 minutes. Pour over crust. Sprinkle with walnuts. Bake 30 to 35 minutes or until filling is set. Cool completely in pan. Cut into bars. Store in refrigerator.

*Makes 24 bars*

*Quick Chocolate Softies*

## Spicy Oatmeal Raisin Cookies

1 package **DUNCAN HINES®
   Moist Deluxe® Spice Cake
   Mix**
4 **egg whites**
1 **cup uncooked quick-
   cooking oats (not instant
   or old-fashioned)**
½ **cup vegetable oil**
½ **cup raisins**

*1.* Preheat oven to 350°F. Grease cookie sheets.

*2.* Combine cake mix, egg whites, oats and oil in large mixing bowl. Beat at low speed with electric mixer until blended. Stir in raisins. Drop by rounded teaspoonfuls onto prepared cookie sheets.

*3.* Bake 7 to 9 minutes or until lightly browned. Cool 1 minute on cookie sheets. Remove to cooling racks; cool completely.

*Makes 4 dozen cookies*

*Spicy Oatmeal Raisin Cookies*

# Chocolate Cherry Cookies

**1 package (8 ounces) sugar-free low-fat chocolate cake mix**
**3 tablespoons fat-free (skim) milk**
**½ teaspoon almond extract**
**10 maraschino cherries, rinsed, drained and cut into halves**
**2 tablespoons white chocolate chips**
**½ teaspoon vegetable oil**

*1.* Preheat oven to 350°F. Spray baking sheets with nonstick cooking spray; set aside.

*2.* Beat cake mix, milk and almond extract in medium bowl with electric mixer at low speed. Increase speed to medium when mixture looks crumbly; beat 2 minutes or until smooth dough forms. (Dough will be very sticky.)

*3.* Coat hands with cooking spray. Shape dough into 1-inch balls. Place balls 2½ inches apart on prepared baking sheets. Flatten each ball slightly. Place cherry half in center of each cookie.

*4.* Bake 8 to 9 minutes or until cookies lose their shininess and tops begin to crack. Do not overbake. Remove to wire racks; cool completely.

*5.* Heat white chocolate chips and oil in small saucepan over very low heat until chips melt. Drizzle cookies with melted chips. Allow drizzle to harden before serving.          *Makes 20 cookies*

## Magical Tip

*Completely cool all cookies before storing in airtight containers. Store each kind of cookie separately to prevent transfer of flavor and changes in texture.*

# *Enchanting Desserts*

## Brownie Ice Cream Pie

**1 package DUNCAN HINES® Chewy Fudge
   Brownie Mix**
**2 eggs**
**½ cup vegetable oil**
**¼ cup water**
**¾ cup semisweet chocolate chips**
**1 (9-inch) unbaked pastry crust**
**1 (10-ounce) package frozen sweetened sliced
   strawberries**
**Vanilla ice cream**

*1.* Preheat oven to 350°F.

*2.* Combine brownie mix, eggs, oil and water. Stir
with spoon until blended, about 50 strokes. Stir in
chips. Spoon into crust. Bake 40 to 45 minutes or
until set. Cool. Purée strawberries in food processor.
Cut pie into wedges. Serve with ice cream and
puréed strawberries.          *Makes 8 servings*

*Brownie Ice Cream Pie*

## Individual Cheesecake Cups

### Crust

**1 package DUNCAN HINES®
Moist Deluxe® Yellow or
Devil's Food Cake Mix**
**¼ cup margarine or butter,
melted**

### Cheese Filling

**2 packages (8 ounces each)
cream cheese, softened**
**3 eggs**
**¾ cup sugar**
**1 teaspoon vanilla extract**

### Topping

**1½ cups dairy sour cream**
**¼ cup sugar**
**1 can (21 ounces) cherry pie
filling (optional)**

*1.* Preheat oven to 350°F. Place 2½-inch foil or paper liners in 24 muffin cups.

*2.* For crust, combine cake mix and melted ¼ cup margarine in large bowl. Beat at low speed with electric mixer for 1 minute. Mixture will be crumbly. Divide mixture evenly among muffin cups. Level but do not press.

*3.* For filling, combine cream cheese, eggs, ¾ cup sugar and vanilla extract in medium bowl. Beat at medium speed with electric mixer until smooth. Spoon evenly into muffin cups. Bake at 350°F for 20 minutes or until set.

*4.* For topping, combine sour cream and ¼ cup sugar in small bowl. Spoon evenly over cheesecakes. Return to oven for 5 minutes. Cool completely. Garnish each cheesecake with cherry pie filling, if desired. Refrigerate until ready to serve.

*Makes 24 servings*

### Magical Tip

*To melt ¼ cup (½ stick) of margarine or butter, place it in a microwavable measuring cup or bowl. Heat at HIGH 50 to 60 seconds.*

*Individual Cheesecake Cups*

# Rum and Spumone Layered Torte

1 package (18 to 19 ounces) moist butter recipe yellow cake mix
3 eggs
½ cup butter, softened
⅓ cup plus 2 teaspoons rum, divided
⅓ cup water
1 quart spumone ice cream, softened
1 cup whipping cream
1 tablespoon powdered sugar
Candied cherries
Red and green sugars for decorating (optional)

• Preheat oven to 375°F. Grease and flour 15½×10½×1-inch jelly-roll pan. Combine cake mix, eggs, butter, ⅓ cup rum and water in large bowl. Beat with electric mixer at low speed just until moistened. Beat at high speed 4 minutes. Pour evenly into prepared pan.

• Bake 20 to 25 minutes or until toothpick inserted in center comes out clean. Cool in pan 10 minutes. Turn out of pan onto wire rack; cool completely.

• Cut cake into three 10×5-inch pieces. Place one cake layer on serving plate. Spread with half the softened ice cream. Cover with second cake layer. Spread with remaining ice cream. Place remaining cake layer on top. Gently push down. Wrap cake in plastic wrap and freeze at least 4 hours.

• Just before serving, combine cream, powdered sugar and remaining 2 teaspoons rum in small chilled bowl. Beat at high speed with chilled beaters until stiff peaks form. Remove cake from freezer. Spread thin layer of whipped cream mixture over top of cake. Place star tip in pastry bag; fill with remaining whipped cream mixture. Pipe rosettes around outer top edges of cake. Place cherries in narrow strip down center of cake. Sprinkle colored sugars over rosettes, if desired. Serve immediately.

*Makes 12 servings*

*Rum and Spumone Layered Torte*

# Hot Fudge Sundae Cake

**1 package DUNCAN HINES®
Moist Deluxe® Dark
Chocolate Fudge Cake Mix**
**½ gallon brick vanilla ice
cream**

## Fudge Sauce

**1 can (12 ounces) evaporated
milk**
**1¼ cups sugar**
**4 squares (1 ounce each)
unsweetened chocolate**
**¼ cup butter or margarine**
**1½ teaspoons vanilla extract**
**¼ teaspoon salt**
**Whipped cream and
maraschino cherries, for
garnish**

*1.* Preheat oven to 350°F. Grease
and flour 13×9×2-inch pan.
Prepare, bake and cool cake
following package directions.

*2.* Remove cake from pan. Split
cake in half horizontally. Place
bottom layer back in pan. Cut ice
cream into even slices and place
evenly over bottom cake layer
(use all the ice cream). Place
remaining cake layer over ice
cream. Cover and freeze.

*3.* For fudge sauce, combine
evaporated milk and sugar in
medium saucepan. Stir constantly
on medium heat until mixture
comes to a rolling boil. Boil and
stir for 1 minute. Add unsweetened
chocolate and stir until melted.
Beat over medium heat until
smooth. Remove from heat. Stir in
butter, vanilla and salt.

*4.* Cut cake into serving squares.
For each serving, place cake
square on plate; spoon hot fudge
sauce on top. Garnish with
whipped cream and maraschino
cherry.

*Makes 12 to 16 servings*

## Magical Tip

*The hot fudge sauce may be
prepared ahead and refrigerated in
a tightly sealed jar. Reheat it when
you are ready to serve the cake.*

*Hot Fudge Sundae Cake*

## Double Berry Layer Cake

**1 package DUNCAN HINES®
    Moist Deluxe® Strawberry
    Supreme Cake Mix**
**²/₃ cup strawberry jam, divided**
**2½ cups fresh blueberries,
    rinsed, drained and
    divided**
**1 container (8 ounces) frozen
    whipped topping, thawed
    and divided**
**    Fresh strawberry slices, for
    garnish**

*1.* Preheat oven to 350°F. Lightly grease and flour two 9-inch round cake pans.

*2.* Prepare, bake and cool cake following package directions for basic recipe.

*3.* Place one cake layer on serving plate. Spread with ⅓ cup jam. Arrange 1 cup blueberries on jam. Spread half the whipped topping to within ½ inch of cake edge. Place second cake layer on top. Repeat with remaining ⅓ cup jam, 1 cup blueberries and remaining whipped topping. Garnish with strawberry slices and remaining ½ cup blueberries. Refrigerate until ready to serve.

*Makes 12 servings*

## Pumpkin Crunch Cake

**1 package (18.25 ounces)
    yellow cake mix, divided**
**2 eggs**
**1²/₃ cups LIBBY'S® Pumpkin Pie
    Mix**
**2 teaspoons pumpkin pie
    spice**
**⅓ cup flaked coconut**
**¼ cup chopped nuts**
**3 tablespoons butter or
    margarine, softened**

**COMBINE** *3 cups* cake mix, eggs, pumpkin pie mix and pumpkin pie spice in large mixer bowl. Beat on low speed until moistened. Beat on medium speed for 2 minutes. Pour into greased 13×9-inch baking pan.

**COMBINE** *remaining* cake mix, coconut and nuts in small bowl; cut in butter with pastry blender or two knives until mixture is crumbly. Sprinkle over batter.

**BAKE** in preheated 350°F. oven for 30 to 35 minutes or until wooden pick inserted in center comes out clean. Cool in pan on wire rack.     *Makes 20 servings*

*Double Berry Layer Cake*

## Chocolate Chip Cheesecake

**1 package DUNCAN HINES®
Moist Deluxe® Devil's
Food Cake Mix**
**½ cup vegetable oil**
**3 (8-ounce) packages cream
cheese, softened**
**1½ cups granulated sugar**
**1 cup sour cream**
**1½ teaspoons vanilla extract**
**4 eggs, lightly beaten**
**¾ cup semisweet mini
chocolate chips, divided**
**1 teaspoon all-purpose flour**

*1.* Preheat oven to 350°F. Grease 10-inch springform pan.

*2.* Combine cake mix and oil in large bowl. Mix well. Press onto bottom of prepared pan. Bake 22 to 25 minutes or until set. Remove from oven. *Increase oven temperature to 450°F.*

*3.* Place cream cheese in large mixing bowl. Beat at low speed with electric mixer, adding sugar gradually. Add sour cream and vanilla extract, mixing until blended. Add eggs, mixing only until incorporated. Toss ½ cup chocolate chips with flour. Fold into cream cheese mixture. Pour filling onto crust. Sprinkle with remaining ¼ cup chocolate chips.

*4.* Bake 5 to 7 minutes. *Reduce oven temperature to 250°F.* Bake 60 to 65 minutes or until set. Loosen cake from side of pan with knife or spatula. Cool completely in pan on cooling rack. Refrigerate until ready to serve. Remove side of pan.
*Makes 12 to 16 servings*

### Magical Tip

*To prevent the top of the cheesecake from cracking, place a pan of water on the bottom rack of the oven while the cheesecake is baking.*

*Chocolate Chip Cheesecake*